20 THINGS YOU DIDN'T KNOW ABOUT

AMPHIBIAN ADAPTATIONS

SLOANE HUGHES

PowerKiDS
press
New York

Published in 2023 by The Rosen Publishing Group, Inc.
29 East 21st Street, New York, NY 10010

Portions of this work were originally authored by Emily Mahoney and published as *20 Fun Facts About Amphibian Adaptations*. All new material in this edition was authored by Sloane Hughes.

Editor: Amanda Vink
Book Design: Tanya Dellaccio

Photo Credits: Cover Cover (speech bubble) Gohsantosa/Shutterstock.com; cover (logo art) NazArt/Shutterstock.com; cover (frog) Dynamicfoto/Shutterstock.com; p. 5 (newt) DOME PRATUMTONG/Shutterstock.com; p. 5 (frog) Opayaza12/Shutterstock.com; p. 5 (salamander) germantphotography/Shutterstock.com; p. 5 (toad) natthawut ngoensanthia/Shutterstock.com; p. 6 Klaus Ulrich Mueller/Shutterstock.com; p. 7 Jess Lang/Shutterstock.com; p. 8 Dave Denby Photography/Shutterstock.com; p. 9 LouiesWorld1/Shutterstock.com; p. 10 Buddy Mays/Alamy Images; p. 11 Dr Morley Read/Shutterstock.com; p. 12 kyslynskahal/Shutterstock.com; p. 13 Marco Maggesi/Shutterstock.com; p. 14 Radiant Reptilia/Shutterstock.com; p. 15 CampSmoke/Shutterstock.com; p. 16 Marek R. Swadzba/Shutterstock.com; p. 17 Rosa Jay/Shutterstock.com; p. 18 Robert Hamilton/Alamy Images; p. 19 Arm001/Shutterstock.com; p. 20 Mike Wilhelm/Shutterstock.com; p. 21 Taniaaraujo/Shutterstock.com; p. 22 Milan Zygmunt/Shutterstock.com; p. 23 Wirestock Creators/Shutterstock.com; p. 24 worldswildlifewonders/Shutterstock.com; p. 25 Valerio Pardi/Shutterstock.com; p. 26 Matej Ziak/Shutterstock.com; p. 29 William Cushman/Shutterstock.com.

Library of Congress Cataloging-in-Publication Data
Names: Hughes, Sloane, author.
Title: 20 things you didn't know about amphibian adaptations / Sloane Hughes.
Other titles: Twenty things you didn't know about amphibian adaptations
Description: New York : PowerKids Press, [2023] | Series: Did you know?
   animal adaptations | Includes index.
Identifiers: LCCN 2021052208 (print) | LCCN 2021052209 (ebook) | ISBN
   9781538386712 (library binding) | ISBN 9781538386699 (paperback) | ISBN
   9781538386705 (6 pack) | ISBN 9781538386729 (ebook)
Subjects: LCSH: Amphibians–Adaptation–Juvenile literature. | Adaptation
   (Biology)–Juvenile literature.
Classification: LCC QL644.2 .H83 2023 (print) | LCC QL644.2 (ebook) | DDC
   597.8–dc23/eng/20211118
LC record available at https://lccn.loc.gov/2021052208
LC ebook record available at https://lccn.loc.gov/2021052209

Manufactured in the United States of America

CPSIA Compliance Information: Batch #CSPK23. For Further Information contact Rosen Publishing, New York, New York at 1-800-237-9932.

Find us on

CONTENTS

ASTONISHING AMPHIBIANS

More than 8,000 kinds of amphibians live in places around the world. Amphibians include frogs, toads, salamanders, and newts. Some amphibians live in faraway places, while others might live right in your backyard!

Amphibians need water or a wet **habitat** to survive. Each species has **evolved** with **unique** features called adaptations that help it survive and **thrive** in its **environment**. Let's check out some awesome amphibian adaptations!

NEWT

TOAD

FROG

SALAMANDER

Early amphibians were the first vertebrates to crawl on land around 370 million years ago. Most amphibians still divide their lives between land and water.

FROG FLAIR

If you've ever picked up a frog, you'll know it feels slimy! That's because there's a thin layer of mucus, a thick liquid, on it. That keeps the frog's skin from drying out. In fact, frogs don't drink water. They **absorb** it through areas on their bellies and thighs!

As frogs grow new skin, they get rid of the old outer layer to make sure they stay wet. They do this by ripping off the old skin. Then, they eat it!

When temperatures drop, wood frogs freeze.

When winter comes, a wood frog's body freezes. The wood frog has special **proteins** in its blood, however, that prevent freezing within the cells. When the weather warms up, the wood frog **thaws** out and continues on its way!

A frog's eyes are on top of its head, and those eyes can see in many directions. Frogs have very good eyesight and can even see well in the dark.

It's hard to surprise a frog!

8

DID YOU KNOW?

Frogs use their eyes to help them eat.

Frogs seem to blink when they're eating food. In fact, their eyes sink into their head to help them push food down. Yum!

Some tree frogs have long tongues that are very sticky! They can catch prey that's moving very fast. Their tongue moves five times faster than you can blink. A frog's tongue is usually around one-third the length of the frog's body!

Frogs eat small creatures such as flies, moths, snails, and worms.

Some tree frogs
have sticky feet.

Some tree frogs have super-sticky feet. They can even climb on glass! Their feet have tiny parts scientists call "nanopillars." These parts use mucus to help frogs climb. This helps them stay safe in trees!

DID YOU KNOW?

Tree frogs can beat most other kinds of frogs in a long jump contest!

Tree frogs use their long legs to jump from branch to branch in trees. Their legs are so powerful that the frogs can jump up to 50 times their body length.

Each species of frog has a special mating call. These calls are made by males and usually last up to 30 seconds at a time. Female frogs listen for these calls, and then they pick their mate!

DID YOU KNOW?

The "ribbet" sound we think of frogs making is actually the **mating** call of the Baja California tree frog.

MAD TOAD SKILLS

DID YOU KNOW?

DID YOU KNOW?
Some toads can use their skin to hurt **predators**.

When some kinds of toads feel like they're in danger, they can let out a toxin, or poison, from their skin.

This poison is called bufotoxin. It looks like milky liquid, and it can be harmful to people too!

Toads usually live in dirt, mud, and sand. Many toads are different shades of brown so that they are hard to pick out from their surroundings.

This means they're tricky to find when predators are looking for them. They also have bumpy skin for the same reason.

Amphibians need water to survive, but the Couch's spadefoot toad lives in deserts in the United States. It uses hard body parts called spades on its back feet to dig in the sand. During the driest seasons, it hides underground to conserve, or save, water.

This natterjack toad, like most toads, prefers living in fields or grasslands.

Toad and frogs are both in the same scientific order, Anura. All toads fit in the "frog" group within the order, but the word "toad" is only used for some.

Toads have shorter legs and usually crawl rather than hop. They also have dry, warty skin that holds water better. That allows them to live farther away from wet places.

SNAZZY SALAMANDERS

DID YOU KNOW?
Salamanders can regrow their tails.

If a predator catches a salamander by its tail, it's not over for the salamander. The salamander's tail can **detach** from the rest of its body so it can escape. The tail will regenerate, or grow back, later.

The axolotl, a type of salamander, can regrow a limb multiple times.

Mudpuppy salamanders can regrow their tails. They can also regrow their legs and even parts of their brain. Sometimes, a leg starts to grow as another one heals. When that happens, they can wind up with extra legs!

A salamander's bright colors help keep it safe.

Brightly colored animals give predators a clear warning: stay away! The fire salamander has bright yellow markings that warn predators that it's poisonous. Other poisonous salamanders are bright orange or red.

There are about 500 species of salamanders.

DID YOU KNOW?

A spotted salamander lays eggs that are surrounded by a jellylike layer.

Salamanders lay their eggs in masses called egg sacs. These make it more likely that the eggs will be safe from predators and hatch into baby salamanders. These egg sacs are usually attached to plants below water.

NEAT NEWTS

DID YOU KNOW?

Newts are a type of salamander.

While adult salamanders live on land and return to the water to lay their eggs, many newts live much of their lives in the water.

There are over 60 species of newts.

DID YOU KNOW?

Many newts have dark colors so they can't be seen at night.

Some newts are nocturnal, which means they sleep during the day and move around at night. This adaptation helps protect them from being seen by predators.

AMPHIBIAN FEATURES

TOADS

SHORT BACK LEGS

BUMPY, DRY SKIN

LIVE IN DRY ENVIRONMENTS

FROGS

LONG LEGS

HOP OR JUMP

SMOOTH, SLIMY SKIN

ALL AMPHIBIANS

ALL BORN IN THE WATER

COLD-BLOODED

NEWTS

WEBBED FEET

PADDLE-LIKE TAIL

SALAMANDERS

ADULTS LIVE ON LAND

WET SKIN

WELL-DEVELOPED TOES FOR DIGGING IN SOIL

DID YOU KNOW?

Amphibians breathe through their skin.

Amphibians need their skin to stay wet so they can breathe! Tadpoles and some **aquatic** amphibians have gills, and many amphibians have lungs too.

Tadpole gills are located on the inside of their bodies.

ADULT AMPHIBIANS LAY EGGS IN WATER.

LIFE CYCLE OF AN AMPHIBIAN

TADPOLES GROW, AND THEIR BODIES CHANGE INTO FULL-SIZED AMPHIBIANS.

TADPOLES HATCH FROM THE EGGS.

AWESOME ADAPTATIONS!

Aren't amphibians awesome creatures? Since appearing on land so long ago, amphibians have evolved to make their homes all over the world. Their adaptations have helped them thrive in many kinds of environments, including rivers, lakes, and creeks as well as the dry, dusty desert.

Frogs, toads, newts, and salamanders may live in many different places, but they share one important feature: their lives begin in the water! What kinds of other adaptations do amphibians have where you live?

Axolotls live naturally only in a lake in Mexico City.

GLOSSARY

absorb: To take something in or swallow something up.

aquatic: Growing, living, or taking place in water.

detach: To separate from something else or from others, especially for a purpose.

environment: The conditions that surround a living thing and affect the way it lives.

evolve: To grow or change over time.

habitat: The natural home for plants, animals, and other living things.

mate: To come together to make babies.

predator: An animal that hunts other animals for food.

protein: A basic structure made of amino acids and found in all life. There are many different kinds.

thaw: To return to a normal temperature after being frozen.

thrive: To grow successfully.

unique: Special or different from anything else.

vertebrate: An animal that has a backbone.

FOR MORE INFORMATION

BOOKS

Hughes, Catherine. *Little Kids First Big Book of Reptiles and Amphibians.* Washington, D.C.: National Geographic Kids, 2020.

Moffett, Mark W. *Face to Face with Frogs.* London, U.K.: National Geographic Kids, 2019.

WEBSITES

Amphibiaweb

amphibiaweb.org/

Enjoy reading about the amphibian of the week!

Ducksters: Amphibians

www.ducksters.com/animals/amphibians.php

Read about the largest and smallest amphibians and many more facts.

INDEX